focus on

Malaysia

...EWS

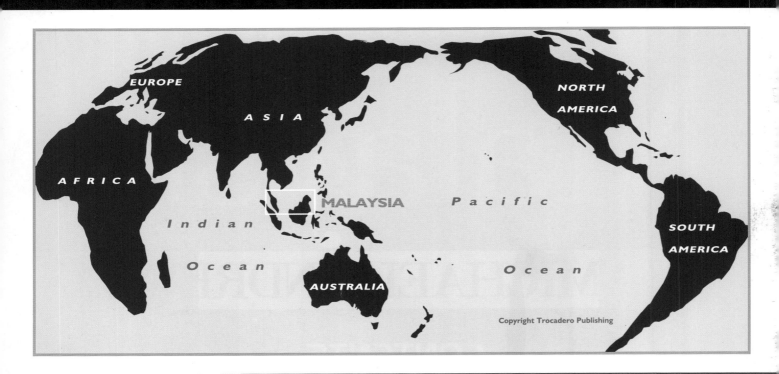

EUROPE

ASIA

NORTH AMERICA

AFRICA

MALAYSIA

Indian

Pacific

SOUTH AMERICA

Ocean

Ocean

AUSTRALIA

Malaysia

THAILAND

SOUTH

CHINA

SEA

Alor Setar

Kota Bahru

Georgetown
Butterworth

Kuala Terengganu

Ipoh

Kuantan

KUALA LUMPUR

Klang

Seremban

Malacca

Johor Bahru

INDONESIA

0   Kilometres   200

Kuching

SINGAPORE

Introduction to Malaysia

Malaysia was created in the 1960s from a group of former British colonies on the Malay Peninsula and the island of Borneo. One of the least populous of all Asian nations, most of its citizens enjoy a relatively high standard of living.

Economic and political stability have encouraged many large corporations to establish factories in Malaysia in the past thirty years.

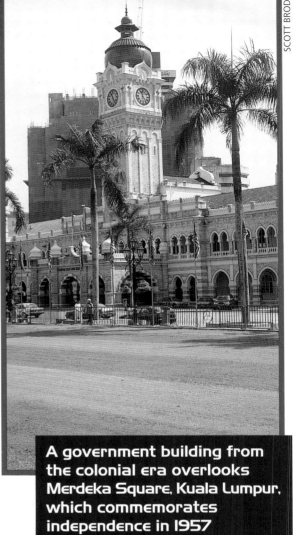

SCOTT BRODIE

A government building from the colonial era overlooks Merdeka Square, Kuala Lumpur, which commemorates independence in 1957

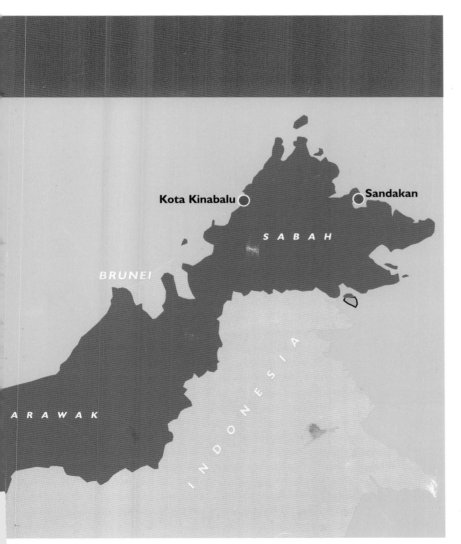

Kota Kinabalu

Sandakan

SABAH

BRUNEI

ARAWAK

INDONESIA

Major investments have been made in key infrastructure such as roads, public transport and airports. However, the government does tend to invest heavily in grandiose projects with marginal chances of profitability.

The population is predominantly indigenous Malay, with significant Chinese and Indian minorities. The 1957 constitution gives the Malay population special privileges not available to the rest of the people. Even so, Malaysia is one of the more successful examples of transition from European colonialism to independence.

Government structure

Country name
Malaysia
Government type
Constitutional monarchy
Capital
Kuala Lumpur
Head of state
Yang Dipertuan Agong
(Paramount Ruler)
Head of government
Prime Minister
Cabinet
Appointed by the Prime Minister from among elected members of the Parliament
Legislative branch
Parliment (Parliament) comprising Dewan Rakyat (House of Representatives) — lower house, members elected for five-year term Dewan Negara (Senate) — upper house, members appointed by Yang Dipertuan Agong and state Parliaments for six-year terms
Administrative divisions
13 negeri-negeri (states)
2 wilayah-wilayah persekutuan (federal territories)
National holiday
Malaysia Day — 13 August (independence in 1957)
Constitution
31 August 1957; amended 16 September 1963
Legal system
Based on English common law
Voting
21 years of age, universal, non-compulsory

Unlike most former colonies, Malaysia has retained, basically unchanged, the system of government left to it by Britain. It is a parliamentary democracy on Westminster lines.

The head of state holds office on a unique rotating system. Within Malaysia there are nine royal states:

The heart of modern Malaysia — parklands and office buildings at Kuala Lumpur City Centre

Kedah, Perlis, Terengganu, Perak, Kelantan, Pahang, Selangor, Negeri Sembilan and Johor. Each of these is led by a hereditary ruler, or sultan. Every five years one of these sultans takes a turn at being Yang Dipertuan Agong (paramount ruler).

The Dewan Negara (Senate) is the upper house of Parliament. Members are not elected to the sixty-nine seats. Instead, the Yang Dipertuan Agong appoints forty-three members, and each of the thirteen negeri-negeri (states) appoints two.

The Dewan Rakyat (House of Representatives) is elected by the people, voting in 177 geographically based electorates. The structure of electorates is weighted to favour indigenous Malay voters.

The constitution spells out certain special privileges granted to Malays in 1957. These include preferential access to civil service appointments. Further amendments were made in 1972 to increase Malay participation in commerce. The monarch could never come from the Chinese or Indian community.

The original nine sultanates are now states within the Malaysian federation. The other, non-royal, states are Melaka (Malacca), Pinang (Penang), Sabah and Sarawak. Heads of state of these four are appointed by the national government. Sabah and Sarawak retain some special rights such as their own controls on immigration. Sabah has twenty seats in the Dewan Rakyat, Sarawak twenty-eight.

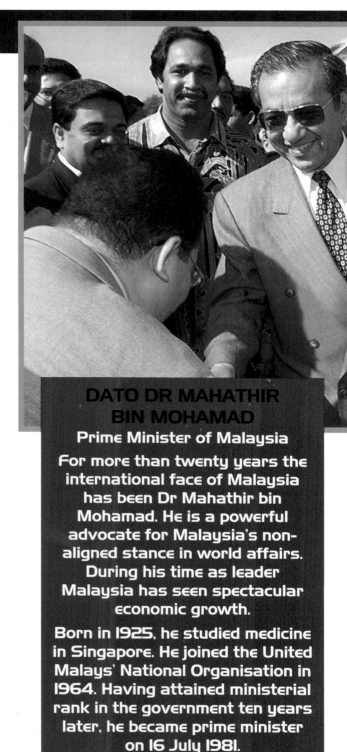

NEWSPIX

DATO DR MAHATHIR BIN MOHAMAD

Prime Minister of Malaysia

For more than twenty years the international face of Malaysia has been Dr Mahathir bin Mohamad. He is a powerful advocate for Malaysia's non-aligned stance in world affairs. During his time as leader Malaysia has seen spectacular economic growth.

Born in 1925, he studied medicine in Singapore. He joined the United Malays' National Organisation in 1964. Having attained ministerial rank in the government ten years later, he became prime minister on 16 July 1981.

WWW.SOURCES

www.smpke.jpm.my
Prime Minister's website

mcsl.mampu.gov.my
Malaysian Civil Service site

www.statistics.gov.my
Statistics about Malaysia

Transport

An air-conditioned minibus waits for passengers

Public transport

For decades the bus has been the main mode of public transport throughout Malaysia. Today the situation is basically unchanged. Modern buses, many air-conditioned, operate services in cities and towns. A system of minibus networks serve less heavily populated areas.

The past ten years have seen a major program of development for public transport in Kuala Lumpur. As well as upgrading bus services, new heavy- and light-rail systems are being constructed. In the more densely populated areas these generally run on elevated tracks, supported by pylons in the centre of roadways.

A taxi queue in Kuala Lumpur

The heavy railway system is operated by the government-owned Keratapi Tanah Melayu (KTM). The suburban network uses a combination of newly created tracks and pre-existing lines. It provides high-quality transport in air-conditioned, modern rail cars.

The Light Rail Transit network is operated by a private consortium called PUTRA. Using ultra-modern technology, it operates and is expanding its 29-kilometre network. The lines cover the eastern and western suburbs of Kuala Lumpur. Mostly they radiate

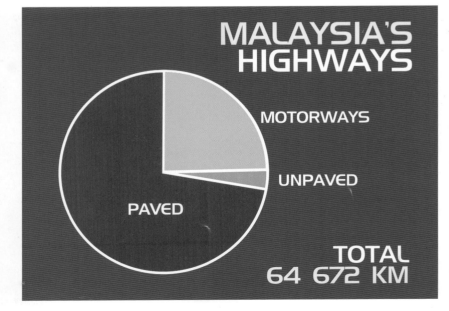

MALAYSIA'S HIGHWAYS

MOTORWAYS

UNPAVED

PAVED

TOTAL 64 672 KM

A suburban commuter bus

from the city centre area to suburban residential and industrial regions.

Also privately owned is the KL Monorail. Scheduled to open in mid-2002, its construction was delayed by the 1997–98 economic crisis. Monorail trains run over a two-way track system for almost nine kilometres in central Kuala Lumpur.

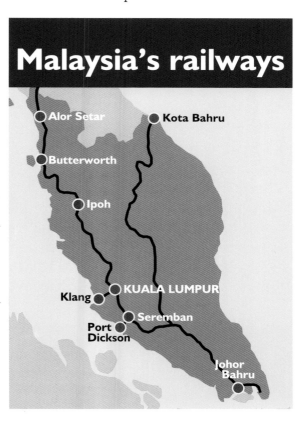

Malaysia's railways

Alor Setar
Kota Bahru
Butterworth
Ipoh
KUALA LUMPUR
Klang
Seremban
Port Dickson
Johor Bahru

Rail

Like most former British colonies, railways played an important part in Malaysia's development. The original line, running thirteen kilometres from Taiping to Port Weld, opened in 1885.

Long-distance rail services were operated until independence by the Federated Malay States Railways (FMSR). Malayan, then Malaysian, Railways was the operator until KTM was created in 1992. Wholly government owned, it operates on a fully commercial basis.

Probably the most famous aspect of Malaysia's railways is the splendid Kuala Lumpur station. Completed in 1917, it was designed by a British architect. It is a wondrous collection of styles: primarily Moorish, there are also Ottoman and Mogul influences, not to mention hints of Gothic and traces of ancient Greece.

A Kuala Lumpur commuter train

TEL : 03-2612 5000
www.takafulnasional.com.my
Nasional

roads. Linking the mainland with the island of Penang is a splendid road bridge constructed in the 1980s.

Kuala Lumpur boasts a major motorway network. It makes the city's traffic more tolerable than most other Asian cities. In older settlements, such as Georgetown on Penang, and Malacca, streets are narrow and can be heavily congested. Kuala Lumpur has some areas, particularly in the old centre, that are clogged with traffic.

Motorcycles are a popular and cheap form of transport in Malaysia

Aviation

Domestic air services are particularly important in linking eastern and western Malaysia. Malaysia Airlines flies between the two and operates domestic routes on the peninsula. It also has a network linking smaller centres in the rugged terrain of Sabah and Sarawak. Most services radiate from Kuala Lumpur, the busiest being

Road

One of the most striking things about Malaysia is the extent and quality of its motorways. From the Johor Causeway in the south to the Thai border in the north, a superb toll road runs the full length of the country. Connected to it are numerous other freeways and toll

www.sources

www.searchmalaysia.com/html/Transportation/Railway
Links to Malaysian railway operators

www.klia.com.my
Kuala Lumpur International Airport site

www.malaysiaairlines.com.my
Malaysia Airlines official site

MALAYSIA'S SHIPPING FLEET

Bulk	62
Cargo	110
Chemical tanker	35
Container	60
Liquefied gas	20
Livestock carrier	1
Passenger	2
Petroleum tanker	58
Refrigerated cargo	1
Roll-on roll-off	6
Specialised tanker	1
Vehicle carrier	6

SCOTT BRODIE

Posting boxes in a city street

Radio is heavily entertainment oriented. Television broadcasts mostly light entertainment, interspersed with patriotic nationalist ceremonies and events. In recent times international news organisations such as BBC World and CNN have been permitted to broadcast on cable television.

During the 1990s Malaysia promoted itself heavily as the multimedia centre of Asia. Prime Minister Mahathir closely identified himself with the push to develop Cyberjaya. This is a multimedia city near Kuala Lumpur in which high-technology companies were encouraged to invest. The collapse of most such enterprises in the late 1990s has left Cyberjaya with a limited future. The internet is very popular with Malaysians. More than ten per cent of the population use it regularly.

Most merely broadcast straight news without comment or any semblance of investigative reporting. Broadcaster TV3 is owned by the UMNO political organisation.

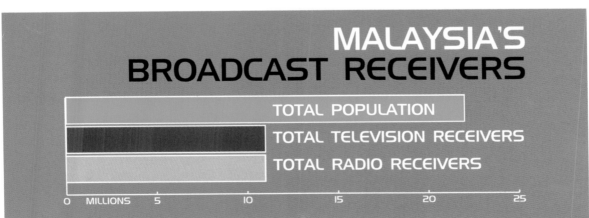

MALAYSIA'S BROADCAST RECEIVERS

| TOTAL POPULATION |
| TOTAL TELEVISION RECEIVERS |
| TOTAL RADIO RECEIVERS |

0   MILLIONS   5   10   15   20   25

Industry: primary and secondary

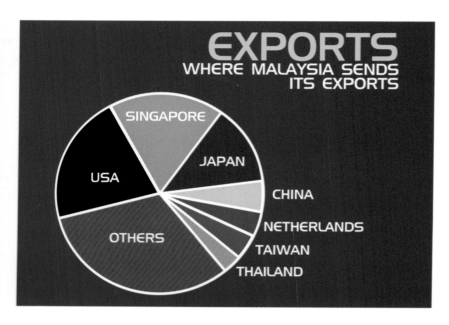

EXPORTS
WHERE MALAYSIA SENDS
ITS EXPORTS

- SINGAPORE
- JAPAN
- CHINA
- NETHERLANDS
- TAIWAN
- THAILAND
- OTHERS
- USA

At the time of independence Malaysia's economy relied heavily on agriculture and mining. Tin, rubber and palm oil provided a significant slice of the country's revenue. All these enterprises were controlled by investors in London. Since that time ownership has gradually shifted to Malaysia.

An aggressive program of promoting Malaysia to manufacturers in Japan, Europe and North America was begun. It resulted in a wide range of manufacturing enterprises setting up in new industrial estates.

MALAYSIA'S MAIN SECONDARY INDUSTRIES
rubber, palm oil processing and manufacturing, light manufacturing industry, electronics, tin mining and smelting, logging and processing timber, petroleum refining

Malaysia still derives considerable revenue from primary industries. Palm oil and rubber retain their importance, as does tin mining. In Sabah harvesting high-quality timbers is a major industry. The extent of logging has resulted in protests by conservationists. Both Sabah and Sarawak have substantial oil industries, both drilling and refining.

Manufacturing activity is mostly located in peninsular Malaysia, particularly in Selangor and Penang. Key manufacturing industries are electronics and related components.

Many international corporations have established operations in Malaysia

MALAYSIA'S EXPORTS
US$98 billion
Main exports
electronic equipment, petroleum, liquefied natural gas, chemicals, palm oil, timber, wood products, rubber, textiles

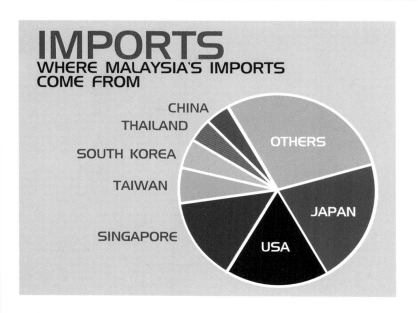

IMPORTS
WHERE MALAYSIA'S IMPORTS COME FROM

- CHINA
- THAILAND
- SOUTH KOREA
- TAIWAN
- SINGAPORE
- OTHERS
- JAPAN
- USA

The engine manufacturing plant for Proton cars

MALAYSIA'S IMPORTS
US$83 billion
Main imports
machinery, transport equipment, chemicals, food, fuel, lubricants

Many household and industrial electrical products are also manufactured in Malaysia.

The government established the EON automobile manufacturing project in the 1980s. It has meant the construction of substantial heavy engineering plants to build bodies, engines and components for the range of Proton cars.

The 1997–98 Asian economic crisis severely affected Malaysia. Although refusing International Monetary Fund support, the country had to resort to tight controls on currency movement and capital markets.

A substantial number of development projects were halted. In Kuala Lumpur unfinished and abandoned construction sites for office blocks and international hotels became commonplace. The economy is recovering steadily, but many foreign investors continue to be wary. One reason is the continuing control over exchange rates. The Malaysian currency is pegged to the US dollar.

MALAYSIA'S MAIN PRIMARY INDUSTRIES
rubber, palm oil, cocoa, rice, timber, coconuts, pepper

WWW.SOURCES
www.lgm.gov.my
Links to information about the rubber industry

www.eon.com.my
Proton car site

www.corporateinformation.com/ mysector/Electronics.html
Information on Malaysia's electronics industry

Geography, environment and climate

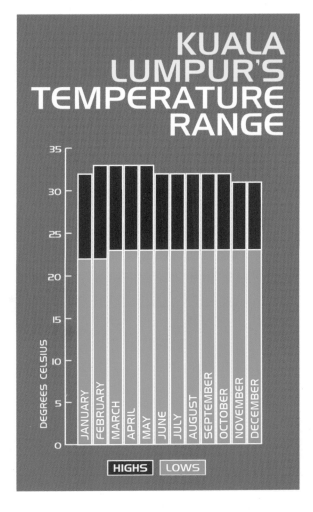

KUALA LUMPUR'S TEMPERATURE RANGE

Chart: Degrees Celsius (0–35) by month — January through December, showing HIGHS and LOWS.

HIGHS **LOWS**

MALAYSIA'S LOCATION
Latitude   2°30'N
Longitude 112°30'E

peninsula is marked by rugged mountain ranges running north to south.

Eastern Malaysia comprises Sarawak and Sabah, located on the northern portion of the island of Borneo. They are known for their rugged terrain and thick jungles. The country's highest mountain, Gunung Kinabalu (4100 metres), is in Sabah.

Malaysia is in the tropical zone. The primary climatic influences are the south-west monsoon from April to October and the north-east monsoon for the rest of the year. The coastal

Malaysia is two distinct geographic entities. Western, or peninsular, Malaysia is an 800-kilometre long strip of land. It extends from the Thai border in the north to the Johor Strait at Singapore in the south. The spine of the

MALAYSIA'S SIZE
Total area
328 550 sq. km
Coastline **4675 km**
Border countries
Thailand, Indonesia,
Singapore, Brunei

A tropical storm gathers around Kuala Lumpur buildings

plains are generally hot and humid, and rainfall is frequent and heavy.

In contrast to the coast, highland areas in peninsular Malaysia provide a cool respite from the humidity. They include the Genting Highlands, Cameron Highlands and Penang Hill.

MALAYSIA'S LAND USE

- ARABLE LANDS
- CROPS
- FORESTS & WOODLANDS
- OTHER

0% 10 20 30 40% 50 60 70 80%

Water is polluted in some areas as a result of the discharge of untreated sewage. Exhaust emissions from heavy traffic in major centres such as Kuala Lumpur, Johor and George-town cause atmospheric pollution. The excessive cutting of natural forests has caused land degradation in jungle regions.

KUALA LUMPUR'S RAINFALL

300
250
200
150
100
50
0

millimetres

JANUARY FEBRUARY MARCH APRIL MAY JUNE JULY AUGUST SEPTEMBER OCTOBER NOVEMBER DECEMBER

A riverside village on the north-western coast of peninsular Malaysia

LOCHMAN TRANSPARENCIES — HANS AND JUDY BESTE

Most were developed as resorts or hill stations during the colonial days.

Most of Malaysia's natural hazards are as a result of its rainfall. Flooding is common in many areas. The downpours can also cause severe landslides and subsidence. Fortunately earthquakes and volcanic activity are not a problem.

While not as severe as in other Asian countries, Malaysia does have considerable environmental problems.

www.sources

www.travel.com.hk/malaysia/weather.htm
Climatic conditions for Malaysia

geography.about.com/library/maps/blmalaysia.htm
Links to sites about Malaysian geography

www.jas.sains.my/doe/egfirst.htm
Department of Environment, many links

Peoples and daily life

MALAYSIA'S ETHNIC MIX

INDIAN

CHINESE

OTHERS

MALAY

is in the hands of Chinese-Malaysians. This makes them the wealthiest group in the community, and is a major source of racial tension.

Indians are a significant minority in peninsular Malaysia. Most are descended from indentured Tamil labourers brought in by British colonists to work on rubber plantations in the late

An open-air mall with many shops and cafés in central Kuala Lumpur

The original people of Malaysia were ethnically Malay. They migrated south from China 4000 years ago. In Sarawak and Sabah the Iban are the indigenous people. Today, in both these regions, they remain the dominant ethnic grouping. Peninsular Malaysia has also been influenced by immigration from India and the Indonesian archipelago.

The next largest ethnic group in both sections of the country is the Chinese. They began arriving around 500 years ago as trade grew in importance. Most of Malaysia's commerce

nineteenth century. Today a large section of Malaysia's smaller commercial enterprises is run by Indian families.

At independence life for most Malaysians centred on manual or agricultural work. Today a large portion of the population is engaged in manufacturing or service work. The nation has become a major manufacturing centre

MALAYSIA'S POPULATION
TOTAL 22 240 000

AGED 0–14 YEARS

AGED 15–65 YEARS

AGED 65+ YEARS

| 0% | 10 | 20 | 30 | 40% | 50 | 60 | 70 | 80% |

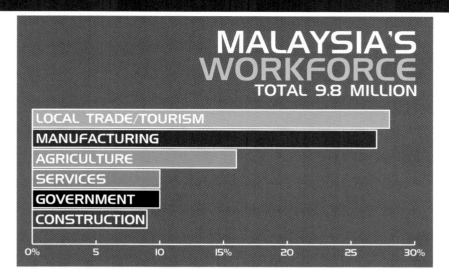

MALAYSIA'S WORKFORCE
TOTAL 9.8 MILLION

LOCAL TRADE/TOURISM						
MANUFACTURING						
AGRICULTURE						
SERVICES						
GOVERNMENT						
CONSTRUCTION						
0%	5	10	15%	20	25	30%

in Asia. Its peoples are skilled in jobs related to the manufacture of high-technology goods, electronics, electrical goods and computer equipment. Most employees work Monday to Saturday, with a half day on Saturday. Muslim devotees take Friday mornings off to attend weekly prayers.

Typical suburban housing in Malaysia

Malaysia's relatively small population means the nation feels much less crowded. Kuala Lumpur, despite rapid growth, can still boast plenty of green open space. It has a quality of life not available elsewhere in Asia. Many Malaysians live in bungalows or terraced housing in quiet suburbs. Overall, Malaysians enjoy one of the highest standards of living in the region.

However, the small size of Malaysia's population has always concerned the government. It is seen as limiting the labour force available to foreign investors. During the 1990s Dr Mahathir declared his aim was to more than double the population to fifty million by the mid-twenty-first century. Most observers believe this is unlikely. Many Malaysians are concerned at the effect it would have on their way of life.

Religion and beliefs

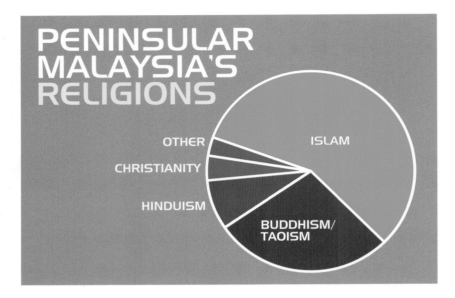

PENINSULAR MALAYSIA'S RELIGIONS

- OTHER
- CHRISTIANITY
- HINDUISM
- ISLAM
- BUDDHISM/ TAOISM

The Masjid Jamek, Malaysia's oldest mosque

SCOTT BRODIE

Malaysia is one of the two east Asian nations with a majority Islamic population. The other is Indonesia. Its dominance can be traced back to 1444 when Muzaffar Shah became sultan of Malacca. He had converted to Islam following the introduction of teachings to Malaya by traders from the Middle East. The subsequent expansion of his domain to cover most of the peninsula resulted in most of the population converting to Islam.

Today Islam is the official state religion. However, Malaysia is not an Islamic state and does not have an Islamic legal code. There is an Islamic political party, but it remains in a minority in the national Parliament. However, it does control some state governments.

Christianity arrived at Malacca in the early sixteenth century with Francis Xavier, shortly after the conquest by Portugal. However, Islam was too well entrenched for it to gain a major hold.

The other two prominent religions are Buddhism and Hinduism. Buddhism's adherents are mainly from the Chinese-Malaysian population, while Hinduism is the religion of many Indian-Malaysians. There is also a small Sikh community.

Despite Islam's status as state religion, freedom of worship is guaranteed under the constitution. Although industry has a Monday to Saturday working week, Muslims are permitted to take Friday mornings off to attend prayers at their mosques.

Food and cuisine

Rice is the key component of any Malaysian meal. The most common ingredients are seafood, poultry and vegetables. The national cuisine is a hybrid of influences from all over Asia. There are traditional Malay meals along

A typical Malaysian restaurant

SCOTT BRODIE

with foods of China — particularly Cantonese — and the hot curries of southern India. Coconut milk is widely used.

Although many dishes are described as national, they vary from state to state. Often only the name remains the same, as tastes and flavours are varied according to local preferences. Foods are prepared in the home and are also widely available at street stalls, in cafés and in restaurants, from the most humble to the grandest.

MALAYSIAN FOODS

Satay
marinated pieces of beef, mutton or chicken skewered on bamboo strips, barbecued and served with a peanut (satay) sauce
Nasi Lemak
rice dish cooked in coconut milk
Roti Canai
pancake made from wheat-flour dough
Nasi Dagang
rice and fish curry
Nasi Goreng
fried rice with meat, prawns, egg and vegetables
Rojak
pineapple, cucumber, bean curd, prawn fritter and boiled egg salad
Char Kway Teow
stir-fried rice noodles, minced garlic, prawns, bean sprouts, cockles and eggs
Chicken Rice
chicken with rice cooked in chicken stock
Curry Laksa
noodles in curry
Rendang
slow-cooked meat, coconut milk, chillies, onions and spices

WWW.SOURCES
www.stayfinder.com/travelguide/malaysia/generalinfo/malaysia_cusine.asp
General information on Malaysian cuisine

www.asianinfo.org/asianinfo/culinary/food/malaysia.htm
Malaysian recipes and ingredients

Arts and crafts

LOCHMAN TRANSPARENCIES — JOHN BUTLER

Creating fine batik cloth in Penang

Malaysian arts and crafts are many and varied. Unique and interesting is the hand-crafting of keris, the wavy-bladed knives the region is famous for. The hilts of the knives are superbly crafted by artisans. The skills of the craft are passed down from fathers and grandfathers.

Songket is a special fabric, sometimes called the cloth of gold. It involves using silk for the horizontal weaving pattern and interlacing it with gold or silver thread vertically. These beautiful designs are usually woven on traditional looms.

Superb woodcarving and kite-making are other traditional crafts still practised. Traditional kites are created laboriously by hand, taking up to two months to complete.

Although more usually associated with Indonesia, Wayang Kulit is a traditional Malaysian form of entertainment. It involves the making of intricate shadow puppets that are displayed behind a backlit screen. Puppeteers act out tableaux based on traditional Malay stories.

Malaysia produces some of the world's best batik cloth. The finest examples are made of silk. Designs can printed with a stamping tool or painted directly onto the cloth.

WWW.sources

www.unimas.my/faca/art/Faridah.html
Details of various crafts

www.asia-art.net/batik.html
The story of batik

www.geographia.com/malaysia/performarts.html
Links for arts, craft, drama, dance, etc.

Wayang Kulit puppets

History and politics

Early history

The first settlement of the Malay Peninsula began about 4000 years ago when peoples from China made their way to the region. For close to 2000 years they lived a mostly village-based lifestyle before having much contact with the larger world.

The first traders arrived from India 2300 years ago. The Malay Peninsula was strategically located on the sea route between India and Sumatra and Java, and also on the route to China. Before long a number of important settlements such as Langkasuka, with strong Hindu traditions, had been established. Subsequently, Chinese visitors introduced Buddhism.

Invaders and conquerors

Around AD 750 the powerful Sumatran Hindu kingdom of Srivijaya was expanding. Its bases on the Malay Peninsula soon became successful strategic trading centres. By the ninth century Srivijayan settlements in Kedah and Pattani had assumed almost as much importance as the kingdom's capital at Palembang.

In the eleventh century Malaya was invaded by Chola peoples from India's Coromandel Coast. They ejected Srivijaya and controlled the region for more than fifty years. Srivijaya returned in around 1100 and remained for the next two hundred years.

At the end of the thirteenth century the Siamese Sukhothai kingdom

The Straits Settlements

PENANG

MALACCA

SINGAPORE

exploited Srivijaya's imminent collapse to gain extra territory. Similarly Melayu, the other major Sumatra-based kingdom, occupied the southern part of the Malay Peninsula.

Within a century Malays found themselves under the control of the Hindu Majpahit empire from Java. The Siamese kingdom of Ayutthaya also held some territory in the north.

Malacca and Islam

At the end of the fourteenth century Iskandar Shah, a Majpahit prince, failed in a bid to establish his own state at Singapore. Instead, he created Malacca on the shores of the strait that lay between Malaya and Sumatra. It soon became a prominent trading port.

SCOTT BRODIE

Francis Light, founder of the Prince of Wales Island settlement

Following Iskandar Shah's death a struggle ensued to succeed him. The winner, in 1444, was Muzaffar Shah, an enthusiastic convert to the Muslim faith. He swiftly made Islam the state religion. Within a short time Muzaffar's Malacca had expanded to control most of the Malay Peninsula and some territory on Sumatra.

The Portuguese and the Dutch

A force led by the Portuguese mariner Alfonso de Albuquerque captured Malacca in 1511, forcing the sultan to flee to Johor. With the Portuguese came Christianity in the form of Francis Xavier. However, his success was limited, Islam having already gained a great hold.

Portuguese Malacca was under constant attack from Johor and the sultan, who wanted his territory back. The Dutch, keen to lock the Portuguese out of the lucrative spice trade, formed an alliance with Johor, taking Malacca in 1641.

Their primary interest was using it as a fortress to control traffic through the strait. During the period of war and turmoil in Europe from 1795 to 1818, the Dutch government-in-exile in London requested Britain to occupy Malacca. It was formally ceded to Britain in 1824.

Immigrations and invasions

During the fifteenth century the Minangkabau people of Sumatra established a settlement inland from Malacca. Unlike most such moves in Malayan history, it was achieved without bloodshed.

In the later part of the seventeenth century, the Bugis people from Sulawesi settled in the Selangor region. They developed a thriving trade mining tin. In 1721 they invaded and captured Johor and Riau and extended their influence to Kedah and Perak.

King Rama I of Siam vigorously expanded his territories. In 1816 he gained control of Kedah, Perak, Terengganu and Kelantan.

The Straits Settlements

In 1786 Francis Light was dispatched by the British East India Company to establish a base on the western coast of Malaya. From the Sultan of Kedah he secured Prince of Wales Island (now Penang).

Following the establishment of its trading centre at Singapore in 1819, Britain controlled the Malacca Strait. The three ports — Prince of Wales Island, Malacca and Singapore — were grouped together as the Straits Settlements in 1826. East India Company administration lasted until 1858, when the British government took direct control.

The White Rajas

Thirty-five-year-old James Brooke, a former soldier in the British East India Company, arrived on the northern shores of Borneo in the 1830s seeking adventure. Brooke brought peace to the warring tribes and cleaned up the piracy that was rife on the northern Borneo coast.

The grateful Sultan of Brunei appointed him raja (governor) of Sarawak in 1841. He held the position until his death in 1868, when it passed to his nephew. Sarawak became a British protectorate in 1888, but the Brookes were left to run it much as they had always done.

The Chinese

British occupation attracted immigrants from China. They set up businesses on Prince of Wales Island and in Malacca. Many became very wealthy, founding substantial trading houses.

Others moved inland, leasing tin mines from the sultans. They introduced more efficient extraction methods and brought in Chinese labourers.

Within the Chinese community there was much friction. The twenty years from 1855 saw many bitter feuds, mostly over gambling debts. Revenge killings were commonplace.

A chaotic time

There were many disputes and even wars between the various Malay communities. And there was no love lost between the Malays and the Chinese. The Malays particularly resented the economic power of the Chinese. As well, the great increase in trade along the coast attracted bands of pirates preying on merchant ships.

By the 1870s the battles and feuds were disrupting trade. Merchants with large investments in the region called on Britain to intervene. London also feared the Germans or French would use the disorder to secure territory in Malaya.

The British governor's residence at Georgetown, Penang

SCOTT BRODIE

Securing the peninsula

Britain's solution was to negotiate treaties with the various sultanates. The first, Perak, accepted British support and protection in 1874. In return the sultan permitted an official British 'Resident' in his territory. Although they had no legal powers, before long the residents were de facto colonial governors. Soon Selangor, Pahang and Negeri Sembilan concluded treaties.

Other sultans were less enthusiastic about British control. However, in 1885 Johor signed a treaty of alliance. These five sultanates were grouped together as the Federated Malay States in 1896, with a central government at Kuala Lumpur. Power had effectively passed to the British.

The other four sultanates that today are part of Malaysia came under British control in 1909. Terengganu, Perlis, Kedah and Kelantan had, until then, been part of Siam. The British now controlled the nine states plus the Straits Settlements. By this time the region was commonly referred to as Malaya.

Economic development

With stability now ensured, the federation could move forward. The tin-mining process was mechanised, greatly increasing its output. Of particular importance was the cultivation of rubber and palm oil.

Originally Brazil had a monopoly on rubber production. During the nineteenth century rubber plants were smuggled out and some made their way to Malaya. Here, in an ideal environment, they prospered.

Indian labourers

To work the rubber and palm oil plantations, large numbers of Indian indentured labourers were recruited. Mainly Tamils from Madras, they arrived in the late nineteenth and early twentieth centuries.

They performed the tedious task of milking rubber trees of their latex. Usually they lived in appalling dormitory accommodation provided by the British employers. Their descendants form one of Malaysia's three dominant ethnic groupings today.

The good life

Between the 1890s and the 1940s life for the British expatriates in Malaya was very good. Most went there in their twenties or thirties with the intention of making a lot of money. They would then retire to Britain when they turned sixty.

The invading Japanese used bicycles to achieve a mobility that stunned the defenders of Malaya in 1941–42

Life was much better than back home. They had servants and their buying power made them a dominant force in the economy. In Kuala Lumpur and Georgetown (Penang) they lived in comfortable bungalows with manicured grounds. For recreation there was no shortage of clubs open only to whites.

War arrives

The good life came to a shocking end in late 1941. Britain, heavily committed to the war in Europe, feared Japan would take advantage and move for control of Malaya and Singapore. British, Australian and Indian troops were shipped to the peninsula. It proved too little, too late.

In December 1941 Japanese troops landed from the sea at Kota Bahru in the far north-east. Royal Australian Air Force fighters retaliated, but were wiped out by superior Japanese aircraft. Through December and January the Japanese relentlessly pushed the Allied troops south.

By February 1942 the Allies had retreated across the Johor Causeway to Singapore, surrendering Malaya to the invaders. The North Borneo, Brunei and Sarawak protectorates all fell to Japanese that same month.

Japanese control

The Japanese divided Malaya racially. The sultans remained in place under strict control. Indians were encouraged to join the Japanese-sponsored Indian National Army (INA), which was fighting with Japanese troops to take Burma. Malays enjoyed more freedoms, but they always knew they were a captive

Allied commander Lord Mountbatten thanks Communist leader Chin Peng for his work against the Japanese

people. European civilians were interned in prison camps under appalling conditions.

The Chinese suffered more than any other group. Most had fiercely supported China when it was invaded by Japan in 1937. Now the Japanese took revenge. Supposed traitors were identified and executed brutally. Others were thrown into prison camps.

New colonialism

When the British returned in September 1945 much had changed. The myth of white superiority had gone forever. Even so, Malaya was vitally important to investors in London. Britain decided to streamline the administration of the colonies.

The Brooke family's control of Sarawak ended in 1946 when it and North Borneo (Sabah) were made full crown colonies. The old Straits Settlements group (Singapore, Malacca and Penang) was broken up.

Most important was the proposal to create the Union of Malaya. Included would be the nine sultanates plus Malacca and Penang.

Opposition to the Union

Long-simmering racial tensions exploded. To minimise problems controlling Malaya, Britain always gave special treatment to the majority Malays.

The Chinese and Indians, while economically strong, took only a minor role in politics. By contrast the

A train derailed by explosives placed on the track by Communist guerrillas

Malays were weak economically, but strong politically. Malays feared that inclusion in the union of Penang and Malacca, with their majority Chinese and Indian populations, would disadvantage them.

In a watered-down version of the original proposal, a federation was created in which each sultanate governed itself. A central government in Kuala Lumpur was headed by a British High Commissioner who controlled Malacca and Penang. Thus the Malays were placated.

Malayan Emergency

Full independence, the next logical step, was delayed by the declaration of a state of emergency.

It was sparked off on 16 June 1948 by terrorists killing four people in Perak and one in Johor.

Of the guerrilla bands that harassed the Japanese, the most effective had been the Chinese-dominated Malayan Communist Party (MCP). Their campaign for independence was masterminded by Chin Peng, secretary-general of the MCP from 1947.

The Malayan Emergency lasted officially until 1960. Britain poured in huge numbers of troops. The communists, once called patriots, were now branded as terrorists. To deny sanctuary to the communists, 500 000 Chinese were resettled into special fortified villages.

The enemy's favoured tactic was to attack isolated police posts and British-owned plantations, then melt back into the jungle. Attacks on trains also became commonplace. They even succeeded in assassinating Britain's High Commissioner, Sir Henry Gurney.

The campaign was a hit-and-miss affair until 1952, when Brigadier Gerald Templer was appointed High Commissioner. He was given overall command of both military and civilian administration. The campaign against the communists became more efficient and the worst was over within two years.

Eventually the communists were pushed into a small enclave near the border with Thailand. A peace treaty was finally signed between the Malaysian government and the MCP in 1989.

Independence moves

By the mid-1950s negotiations to grant independence to Malaya were well under way. However, drafting an acceptable constitution raised serious problems.

The British policy of favouring Malays made racial equality impossible. The politically powerful Malays wanted to ensure any Chinese dominance was minimised or eliminated.

The constitution gave a raft of special privileges to the Malays. Large tracts of land were set aside exclusively for their use. They were also given favoured access to civil service jobs. Malay was designated the national language and Islam the state religion, although religious freedom was guaranteed.

The head of state would be a Malay monarch. Each of the nine sultanates would take a turn at providing the monarch for a five-year term. The country would be a federation with separate state governments.

Merdeka

The Federation of Malaya came into being on 31 August 1957. It joined the Commonwealth of Nations and was given a seat at the United Nations. The parting from imperial control was amicable. Merdeka (independence) had been achieved, although the Chinese and Indian communities had less to be pleased about than the Malays.

The prime minister was Tunku Abdul Rahman, a Malayan prince. He led the Alliance, a grouping of Malay, Chinese and Indian political associations. Born in 1903, he studied law at Cambridge University. As a barrister

he served in the Kedah public prosecutor's department from 1949. His rise in politics was swift, with an appointment to the Legislative Council in 1952. Three years later Abdul Rahman was elected Chief Minister of the federation.

The first move towards self-government had been the election of the lower house of Parliament in 1955. Abdul Rahman, a member of the United Malays' National Organisation (UMNO), had negotiated a coalition with the Malay Chinese Association (MCA) and the Malay Indian Association (MIA). Together they won all but one of the fifty-two seats.

Malaysia

Singapore achieved full self-government in May 1959. Its prime minister, Lee Kuan Yew, believed that Singapore's survival depended on union with Malaya. Tunku Abdul Rahman agreed, fearing

Merdeka celebrations in Kuala Lumpur on 31 August 1957

the development of a powerful Chinese-dominated nation on Malaya's border.

Malaysia, created on 16 September 1963, included Singapore, Malaya, Sabah and Sarawak. The last two were included to balance the majority Chinese population of Singapore. The inclusion of Sarawak and Sabah was a hurried affair; neither had undergone any preparation for independence.

Tunku Abdul Rahman (left) in August 1962, announcing that Britain had agreed to the formation of Malaysia

Konfrontasi

The creation of Malaysia was opposed by Indonesia and the Philippines. Indonesia believed both Borneo colonies were rightfully its own; the Philippines had a long-standing claim to Sabah.

President Sukarno of Indonesia launched his campaign of Konfrontasi (Confrontation). Indonesian troops staged regular sorties into Sarawak and Sabah, and terrorist raids were carried out in peninsular Malaysia. The northern Borneo incursions were repelled by British, Australian and New Zealand troops.

When Sukarno was deposed in 1966 by General Suharto, Konfrontasi ended. Indonesia formally recognised Malaysia in 1967. The Philippines followed suit in 1969.

Singapore separates

In Malaysia, strained Chinese–Malay relations worsened dramatically when Lee Kuan Yew's People's Action Party (PAP) tried to establish itself on the Malay Peninsula. Another Chinese-based party would threaten Abdul Rahman's coalition government.

In Singapore, on 21 July, fighting between Chinese and Malays turned swiftly into a full racial riot. A week later twenty-three people were dead. Rioting erupted again in September.

The PAP persisted in its efforts to build a coalition to rule Malaysia. The UMNO reacted by demanding that PAP back down. When this did not happen, on 6 August 1965 Rahman told Lee that Singapore would have to leave the union. Three days later the Malaysian Parliament voted to separate.

Economic development

In the 1960s Malaysia's economy was heavily dependent on tin mining, rubber growing and palm oil cultivation. Control of these industries remained in the hands of London-based organisations.

The government poured substantial funds into the development of manufacturing. Pig-iron production, ship repair and cement manufacture became strategic industries. Electronic components manufacturers from Japan and Europe were encouraged to invest in factories in new industrial estates.

In the 1980s the Proton motor car project commenced in partnership with Mitsubishi of Japan. Today the Proton range is large, with a significant slice of production being exported.

The new emergency

At the 1969 election four minority parties won sufficient seats to deny the government a two-thirds majority in Parliament. Without this it could not alter the constitution. The campaign had been marked by controversy over education, particularly the use of the English language in teaching.

On 13 May, after riots between Chinese and Malays, a state of emergency was declared. Four days of violence and hundreds of deaths ensued. The National Operations Council, headed by Deputy Prime Minister Tun Abdul Razak, took over running the country until February 1971.

The bumiputra progam

Abdul Rahman was replaced as Prime Minister in September 1971 by Abdul Razak. The Alliance coalition was disbanded and replaced by the Barisan Nasional (National Front). It was less racially inclusive and more concerned with shoring up Malay supremacy.

The government claimed the reason for interracial strife was the disparity of wealth between Chinese and Malays. The New Economic Policy created the bumiputras. New laws ensured these indigenous Malays held thirty per cent equity in all Malaysian companies by 1990. Constitutional amendments made it a crime to question the special privileges of Malays.

The new programs were driven by Abdul Razak. He died in office in January 1976. His successor, Hussein Onn, continued the new policies until his retirement in June 1981.

The Mahathir era

In 1981 the leadership of the governing coalition passed to Dr Mahathir bin Mohamad. He led the coalition to victory in 1982, 1986, 1990, 1995 and 1999. During the 1980s and 1990s he used the Internal Security Act to suppress criticism of the lack of freedoms and human rights in Malaysia.

Mahathir has clashed on numerous occasions with other world leaders. In 1991 he claimed data had been leaked to Western media to undermine the Malaysian economy. He also sees himself as a leader of the non-aligned third-world nations.

Tourism is a key component of Malaysia's economy.

The dramatic Malaysian war memorial sculpture

Grand dreams

During Mahathir's time there have been several grandiose efforts to boost Malaysia's international profile and enhance national pride. Most dramatic is the enormous Petronas Towers in Kuala Lumpur, the tallest office buildings in the world. Unfortunately, much of the office space remains unoccupied five years after construction.

The new international airport at Sepang is superbly designed and a pleasure to use. However, it is so big it appears deserted at many times during the day. Its location, an hour's drive by motorway from Kuala Lumpur, is a major hassle for travellers.

In the mid-1990s the government hatched a plan for Cyberjaya, Malaysia's multimedia city. Here, it was proposed, international and Malaysian corporations would set up high-technology laboratories to exploit the new information superhighway. The collapse of the internet revolution in the late 1990s brought much of this to a halt.

The economic crisis

Malaysia was severely hit by the 1997–98 economic collapse. The government refused assistance from the International Monetary Fund. Instead, it implemented wide-ranging controls on currency trading and capital markets. This won Malaysia no friends in the international financial community. The economy is now substantially improved.

The Anwar crisis

In September 1998 Mahathir's Deputy Prime Minister and heir apparent was Anwar Ibrahim. Anwar was seen internationally as a more moderate voice for Malaysia.

In April 1999 Anwar was sentenced to six years imprisonment for corruption. Protests by his supporters were ruthlessly suppressed by police. The independence of Malaysia's judiciary was questioned internationally.

Despite this, at the general elections of November 1999 Mahathir won another term, although the Islamic Party trebled its seats in Parliament.

www.sources

www.geographia.com/malaysia/timeline.htm
Timelines of Malaysian history

www.kiat.net/malaysia/history.html
Concise history of Malaysia

Statistics

The points of the star and the stripes represent the original fourteen states and colonies that made up Malaysia in 1963 (the flag was not altered after Singapore left the union). The blue represents the multiracial unity of the country and the yellow stands for the monarchy.

Total population
22 240 000
Birth rate
24.7 per 1000 population
Death rate
5.2 per 1000 population
Infant mortality rate
20.3 per 1000 live births
Life expectancy
male 68 years
female 74 years

GDP growth rate 8.6%
GDP per capita US$10 500
GDP by sector
agriculture 14%
industry 44%
services 42%

Government revenues
US$16.4 billion
Government expenditures
US$17.8 billion

Labour force 9.6 million
Labour force by sector
local trade, tourism 28%
manufacturing 27%
agriculture 16%
services 10%
government 10%
construction 9%
Unemployment rate 3% plus

Land area 328 550 sq. km
Lowest point
Indian Ocean — sea level
Highest point
Gunung Kinabalu — 4100 m

Natural resources
tin, petroleum, timber, copper, iron ore, natural gas, bauxite

Primary industries
rubber, palm oil, cocoa, rice, timber, coconuts, pepper
Secondary industries
rubber, palm oil, light manufacturing, electronics, tin mining and smelting, logging, timber processing, petroleum refining

Exports US$98 billion
Major exports
electronic equipment, petroleum, liquefied natural gas, chemicals, palm oil, timber, wood products, rubber, textiles
Imports US$83 billion
Major imports
machinery, transport equipment, chemicals, food, fuel, lubricants

Official language
Bahasa Malaysia
Currency
Malaysian ringgit
Religions
Islam, Taoism, Buddhism, Hinduism, Christianity

Index

Focus on Asia: Malaysia   ISBN 0 86415 433 X
Published by   Franklin Watts 96 Leonard Street London EC2A4XD
Created and produced by Trocadero Publishing   Copyright © 2002 S and L Brodie   Printed in Hong Kong